# A LAND WITHOUT A HOME

and other poems

Vandana

artwork by arthi amaran

INDIA • SINGAPORE • MALAYSIA

ISBN 979-8-89277-232-7

# Contents

# Preface

Several thousands of years ago, humans crafted great epics that ran into volumes. One may imagine that there was very little to do during those long dark nights, perhaps without much lighting. There also appears to have been an abundance of impressive memory prowess that for some reason has evolved its way out of the human mind and into memory cards and backup drives.

Today, the human brain appears to have shrunk. Not just in the ability to memorize tomes and volumes for posterity but also in the ability to craft such masterpieces (with the exception of a few like George R. R. Martin who can't seem to stop writing and keeps us on our toes trying to keep up with his works). Our early literary history is far richer than it is today, although in terms of knowledge and technology we have advanced so much more. Nearly all the cultures revelled in them. Many literary creations weren't even stored as texts but simply passed on in memory. And so, were sadly lost as many cultures and traditions that stored these works were also lost.

If we aren't able to create or memorize large texts, a majority of us seem unable to even read or write adequately. As attention spans shrunk slowly, epics gradually shrunk to novels and poems. Novels to short stories. Short stories to terribly tiny tales. Language in writing has undergone mutations in its new and horrifying mobile messaging dialect.

Even for me, poems were just something painful that was included in the syllabus of a school year.

But then, much much later, they became something more.

# 1. Every Morning I Wake Up and Dress Up

Every morning I wake up and dress up.
First, I open my sack of white clickety-clackety bones.
I lay them out like pieces of a puzzle.
Sometimes, just for fun, I put them this way and that.
It's quite fun to see but often ends in a tussle
when the hat that goes on the head ends up where you sat.
Then come on the muscles and ligaments.
The bones pull up like the sails of a ship.
Am wobbly now but no longer need a sack.
I can move like this and I can move like that.
Only my jaw still goes clickety-clack.
I pack in my essentials, winding in my intestine.
I lay in a liver, a spleen and a lovely red heart.
It's a tight fit, so I bend a curve in the spine.
But without its outer covering, everything starts to fall apart.
So I pad in generous amounts of fleshy fat.
(Am not stingy or very vain, I would rather not be thin.)
And quickly wrap over a gentle lacy skin.

I almost forgot my brains, so I squeeze my eyeballs out splat.

I squish the grey through the sockets right in.

It's time to put in the final touches.

This is more meticulous than you think.

Nails and hair must go all in the right patches.

One tuft in the wrong place can raise an awful stink.

At last, I am ready with all the strappings.

But a colourful layer over it all is a must.

A selection of prisons of your choice,

desires or needs, to adorn or add to your poise.

And I am ready for a brand new day

of new adventures, new beginnings, and a whole new way.

Every night I undress and go to sleep.

The hair and nails drop away here and there.

The cheeks sink in and the skin drops its snare.

Maggots and bugs feed hungrily on the putrid flesh,

the bones crumble and rot away its mesh.

But the memories - cling and stick to another day.

Loves, hates and fears linger pointless and unfettered.

Floating in and out of hazy dreams, unfulfilled and scattered

all waiting for another chance

to leap in and out of life's little dance.
Every night I undress and go to sleep.
The body is gone but the soul - I keep.

## 2. Footsteps in the Forest

Outside the village and across the river,
the dark expanse of the forest stood.
Thick and alive, buzzing with birds,
face hidden in a swaying green hood.

Little wings fluttered and beaks twittered,
the leaves laughed a gentle dew.
Across the branches, a happy murmuring was heard,
the forest was alive, every moment was new.

But no footsteps in the forest stray.
No soul would venture near, they say.
Dangerous and lost, forsaken and feared,
not one from the village to the forest steered.

A forbidden land and an abandoned land.
No paths, no signs, no meandering lanes.
Screams of agony and lost cries, they say,
is all that ever escaped its clutches.

I filled the pots and paused in a dream.
The river stopped to tickle my toes.
Fragrance and sounds, filled my mind unseen.
From heart or river, a yearning arose.

The ends of my *sari* and the last of my *pallu*,
the river pulled and swirled in a game.
Forest and river, eager and awaiting.
Forest and river, called my name.

The branches bent in welcome and the stones pointed a way.
A new path and a familiar path, a path that moulds the feet.
The trees gathered around and muffled the mind.
Diamonds of light danced where the earth and sky meet.

Footsteps in the forest, is all I leave,
pressed leaves and little toe puddles.
The ancients shimmered and old loves twinkled by.
Softly and gently, the light of memory closed its eye.

No husband, no child, no house.
The anklets dumb and my bangles mute.
No lies, no sweat, no riddles, no soot.
Prisons of fear open and the ropes of love untie.

Deeper and deeper, through the forest led.
Deeper and deeper, through the soul's sieve.
Footsteps in the forest, they said,
is all they found of me.

# 3. The Soul

Two travellers
hand in hand
travel far and wide.

Two travellers
one unaware of the other.
Without the other, where the first?

Two travellers
roam the world
each step getting slower.

One falls down dead.
The soul looked down and said,
time to look for another.

And a baby gurgled in the arms of a new mother.

# 4. Don't Tell Her the Secret

Don't tell her the secret!
It's for us to keep.
Hidden away from any light.
Not even if she seeks.

A secret that is hidden.
Yet casts its long shadow.
Heavier than a guilt.
Turning friends into a foe.

A secret when revealed
blazes like a new sun
but without a morning sigh.
It wrenches the heart.
And breaks a storm in the eye.

Don't tell her the secret!
She must never know!
It's for us to keep.
Hide its every glow.
Not even if she seeks.

# 5. The Sea and The Sky

The sea and the sky had an argument.
It was a clash of pure sentiment.
Neither would budge an inch.
Neither could make the other flinch.
And so began a tremendous clash
that made the gentle earth gnash.

The sea surged and heaved mightily.
Tearing at its shores viciously.
Great walls of water rose and crashed.
In rows of endless waves they splashed.
It dipped low, spewing froth and white
and then it rose to an even greater height.
It didn't stop or even pause
as it justified its righteous cause.
It whirled about with every trick.
Till just about everyone felt sick.
It even woke the blind in the deep
from their long slumbering sleep.
And set them about to wonder
what folly brought the sea to blunder!
And what, if anything, it all meant.

And just as you thought it was silent,
it would start again to sizzle and toil
bringing the oceans to a steady boil.

The sky was not one to give way
to a show of tantrum that it could easily sway.
It rolled up every cloud it could muster
into a large and billowy bluster.
Pouring down with torrents of rain
and gales that made each drop strain.
It raged and roared through the night
screeched and howled in deadly spite.
With every thunder that rolled and crashed
angry lightening webs sizzled and slashed.
Striking and blinding as it surged
in a furious rage that was never purged.

Not a thing the land could do
while the brothers fought long and true.
Each with all their right and might
till all their anger was blessed white.
And there was not a say on either side
not a puff of wind or a tiny tide.
And in the years to come after,
the tears slowly melted to laughter.

While the truth seeped into a legend
of how the sea and the sky would never amend.
But not one could ever throw any light
on the reason for that glorious fight.

# 6. The Torch

I remember when it all started.
I was ten and we were in Srinagar.
I heard a noise and my eyelids parted.
In the dim light of the open doorway,
I saw it first - silent, watchful and still.
And in the bright morning, I was really quite ill.

I vowed to have a torch by my side.
And the next time I saw it - silent, watchful and still,
I lit up the room so it could not hide.
I was quick as a butterfly but,
lo! It was gone in a stab.
And all that was left was the room - mundane and drab.

Over the years as time passed
it made a few appearances on solitary nights.
And every time I thought it was the last,
again, it stood - silent, watchful and still.
I grew accustomed to its nightly presence.
And even waited for that dull fluorescence.

The seasons rolled swiftly by.
I never quite knew when the visits stopped.

Youth took its course and there was no time to even sigh.
As youth laughs at petty fears and even true ones,
as it webs its way in one long spin,
and tests of all kinds that the wind blew in.

And soon, came the day when a love was arranged.
And in a splash of colours we were bound
to a life together, with vows exchanged.
We were joined by two more who brought
lunch boxes, bills, and childhood tears,
last-minute shoe polishes and exam fears.

The children arranged their own love and each
left to their own while a long sleep took mine.
And I was left to potter in a house, alone and out of reach,
with time to contemplate memories, remembered and not,
with no shirts to iron, or forms to fill,
and that was when it was back - silent, watchful and still.

My skin had wrinkled and my hair had thinned.
My face was worn, for wont of all seasons,
in ways that nature would never rescind.
And yet it hovered like it had never left.
And yet its presence woke me just the same.
It was as if I was ten and it called my name.

I was determined to see
just what or who it was that shimmered in my room.
Silent and watchful and enticing me.
I closed the curtains and the doors
and simmered at its arrogant familiarity.
I was ready with my torch and a brand-new battery.

In the darkness, I lay in wait,
until sleep tripped my eyes cunningly.
But soon I heard a noise and woke to see my bait.
Hurry! As quick as a snake,
I grabbed the torch and shone it bright,
across the room and into the night.

And at last, I saw my adversary.
It stood - silent, watchful and still.
Soft as a gentle cloud - and not that scary.
Two sides of a mirror, did I or did she beckon now?
"Let go the torch, it is time to go," she said. "It was time we met.
You and I, you see, we have paid each other's karmic debt."

# 7. The Painter

Said the painter one day,
"Many a year I have held the brush
to the stars and colours of May,
to tall trees and streams a gush.

I have many colours and many shades.
My brushes are tall, thin, broad and flat.
On my canvas are flowers and pretty maids,
and a soldier in a tin hat."

"Ah," said the Great Artist, "Surely,
there remains a yearning in my heart.
For in all the world I seek,
them who appreciate my art.

Even now I paint with vigour,
yet the colours they grow dark.
The splatters of red now bigger.
With tired patience, I seek to make my mark."

# 8. Frustration

Frustration is
desire unfulfilled.
And, therefore,
he said wisely,
do not have desires!

Well, I said,
gratefully.
Here is one more.
One to not have
any more.

# 9. Amma

*"knowing yourself is the beginning of all wisdom"*

*– Aristotle*

My amma
made me *dosas*
with blobs of *ghee*.
My amma
stood by
and watched me grow.
She laughed at my poor jokes
and admired my squiggly drawings.
She took my hand.
She took my side.
When none would abide
and lent me saris and blouses
to wear to a school show.
She braided and styled
my hair with pretty ties.
My amma.
My only friend
is gone now.
So now I work the signals.

I work the nights.
Everyday
I remember
my amma who
lost a son
and found a daughter
Everyday
I remember
my amma who
took my changed hand
took my changed side
when none would abide.
Everyday
I remember
my amma.

# 10. An Aberration of the Soul

"Poetry?!"
"Yes, poetry," I said
and I looked at the floor.
"What use are poems?"
He declared.
And there the interview ended.
And I was kindly shown the door.

I stood outside and looked up
at the towering buildings.
Wandering from one to another
peering at windows
hoping for prospects
from dull shaking heads.
Me and my little brother.

"What use is poetry, brother?
Amidst the noise of the working world
said the harassed supervisor.
"Poetry is an abomination.
An aberration of the soul.
One that follows you uninvited,
keeps you up at nights,

a brother that is moonlighted.
Calluses of the fingers we bear
But calluses of the soul are a luxury
only for those rich and fair."

# 11. The Enlightened One

I, the fly,
did live many lives before.
Tossed in fate, trapped by thoughts,
this the last, is a debt of the past.
With knowledge and wisdom,
across the last threshold,
into a shining new kingdom.
To the abode of the Formless,
guided by the Light and,
hearing the one Voice of the Voiceless.
As the pot dashes to the floor,
the debt is paid,
and the fly is no more.

# 12. Little Pearls of Zen

I once met
a little Buddhist monk
who sat in a sunny courtyard
stringing up pearls,
little pearls of zen.

Each little pearl
he would hold
in his tiny fingers
and feel them slow
before he declared
that they were all very zen.

## 13. Emily

My little Emily
visits me every day
to drop a poem
or two.
My little Emily
always has something to say.
Just a small verse
or a line
or two.
And so I comply,
what else can I do?
She has a way
that's quite demanding too.
I write for her
or does she write me?
We really aren't quite sure.
Neither of us could be truer.
Who is holding the pen
and who the hand?
Who's word or thought was that?
Was it an inspiration?

Was it a muse?
Who is indeed to say?
Or am I just a prey?
But down it goes on paper
and when it's all done,
I have another nice poem.
But then I look around
and she is gone.
I thought we had just begun?
O Emily, come back for another one.

# 14. Pompeii

I remember.
I remember that day.
A day that is etched in my memory.
Who could forget that sad legacy?
When the earth rumbled and roared
and the mountain cloud soared.

First came a flash of light.
As bright as the sun.
So bright that it was loud
and the earth vomited a cloud.
And oh! the tremendous sound
that threw us to the ground.
A rumble and a roar
from far across the shore.

We fell to the floor and wept
of pain that we felt
even before we knew why.
It was the sorrow of Pompeii!
We should have been with them
to face together and condemn.

Oh the rage of Vesuvius!
Can a God be more angry?
His own creation, we,
blinded by Apollo,
taken in one swallow.
I remember.
I remember the taste to this day.
The ash that everywhere lay.
My skin holds only scars,
the words have faded in my memoirs,
but my heart holds the gashes,
still raw from those ashes.

I remember.
I remember that day
till my old old age.
The rumble in my bones rage.
The cries in my heart echo.
Guilt as sharp as an arrow.
My wife and daughter at Pompeii
on that fateful August day.

# 15. The Colour Blue

He racked his brain and scratched his chin.
Groaning as if in pain, he paced till he was thin.

Dear me, dear me, a week now past.
Forests, mountains and seas have winds blowing fast.

The seeds are sown, the little buds awakening,
small insects unknown, all ready and playing.

But, alas, dear Wife, without a pleasant sky,
the earth and all its life, in despair shall lie.

She stepped by his side, and patted him on the arm,
I'm sure, my love, you have tried and succeed you will, so be calm.

Dear Wife, can you suggest a colour that's so like you,
from the east to the west, deep and serene in hue?

Looking into Her eyes, He suddenly knew,
that when the moon dies, the sky shall take the colour blue.

# 16. Every Time I Want a Little Quiet

Every time I want a little quiet
I close all the doors and retreat
to that old ancient seat.
It's where up is up and is not down.
It's where right is right and is not wrong.
It's where true is true and not a lie.
And no other twists that make you sigh.

Just a tiny breath in and out.
In a place where no one is about.
Where the only sound is silence.
And is its own true guidance.
Then am back again outside
swimming happily in the tide.

# 17. The Physics of Death

I tapped on the door nervously.
"Come in, come in, my lad,"
called a voice, fervently.
I stepped in without a clue.
In that dim, dusty room, he sat,
old and decades in hue,
surrounded by books and papers stacked.
A dishevelled ancient professor,
as if ready to grandly conjecture
dark magic from those blind old hands,
he cleared his throat and began to lecture.
"All of sciences has harnessed
the energy of sun and light,
all elements, bright or darkest,
and examined all their glorious might.
And yet, one elusive secret remains,
hidden, dark and unseeing,
and we, sadly ignorant of that one domain,
that element that flows in every being.
In every living thing that moves and breathes,
thrives a primordial life energy,

within the body that it sheathes.
O my boy, such a noble discovery!
should surpass every other.
And, o my boy, we would be
yet another Nobel brother!
And therefore, my boy,
let us approach our goal,
with every resource we can employ,
with every intention of knowing that soul.

Those tender phantom shoots
that pervade the universe in every pore,
as it transfigures and transmutes,
from life to death in every spore.
Yet in every death arises
from the furthest frontiers,
new life in various surprises,
and so it was and so life steers.

Let us look death in its eye,
and postulate the life that flows,
derive its equation to the last sigh,
from life to death and the final gallows,
and back again in a full wide circle,
and so, my boy, the thesis of your PhD

is a computation of life's eternal,
and shall be the noble death of me!

So, take out all your instruments,
and observe closely - with your lens.
As we perform, thus, our research,
just once and only once in providence.
Our lab is this, our holy church,
for you alone, to capture every consequence,
record the experiment for posterity,
ensure that you have applied
every science and every faculty."
And so he said and so he died.

Thus was I, a partner in crime.
In closed walls, I now do my solitary time.
I am sorry I never got my PhD.
And death, the elusive bastard, he,
still remained a bloody mystery.

# 18. The Zoo

I go to the zoo every day.
It's just down the street from where I stay.
I go in and out when I want.
Running errands for my aunt.
Because my uncle works in the cobra pit
so in my family, he's a hero and a hit.
I take him hot lunch in a pack
and sometimes an evening snack.
And every time I go in and out,
I look for an animal that's about.
I always stop to say,
"Hello, how are you today?"
To the elephant, tiger or the bear
in its cage or in its lair.
In every prison I have a friend
with whom a little love I spend.
Sometimes all I get is a sad vacant stare.
Their lives are naked and ever so bare.
But then at times I think
in that despondent little blink,
I see a faint hopeful wish.

And just a hint of a tail's swish.

And then one day, an activist came
who thought loudly that cages are lame.
She shouted all over the zoo,
"It's a crime and a cruelty too!"
And off she scampered to gather
points of law about the matter.
And soon, she had a frenzied mob.
"Dissent!" they cried, with one large sob.
They shouted slogans and protested.
They jumped up and down and resisted
all attempts for any discussion.
Screaming of rampant corruption,
they talked of rights and laws and nature
and wanted to release every creature.
"We don't want any chitter-chatter.
Animals Lives Matter!"

Then the zoo was closed one day.
And all the animals were sent away.
One by one to different places.
With new people and new faces.
Some to cages they had never been.
Some to cages they had never seen.

Some to cages that were brand new.
Some to cages that they always knew.
Some to cages that were shiny and bright.
Some to cages that fitted tight.
Some to cages that they wouldn't see.
Some to cages that they just wouldn't be.
I was sad as I didn't get to say
"Hello, how are you today?"
Or give a treat and a final goodbye
and hug the animals with a sigh.
It made me think again a lot
who is in the cages and who is not?
The world is a just another large zoo,
we are animals in it too.

# 19. The Twin and I

*...yet still I long*

*for my twin in the sun...*

Patrick Anderson

*It was difficult to decide which was leading and which was led.*

The Solid Mandala – Patrick White

The twin and I
have long since wandered.
Hand in hand.
Breath with breath.
Scoured the sands.
Sailed the seas.
Roamed the lands,
the mountains and the valleys.

Like railway tracks.
Never to part and never to meet.
The eternal twin
ancient and true.
The other - stuck in pain and mortal spin.
Never the same and never to change.

Like a kite.
Never free and never imprisoned.
The eternal one
never seen and never lost.
The other flailing in shade and sun.
Never alone and never released.

The twin and I
have long but wandered.
Hand in hand.
Breath with breath.
Who is leading whom?
Who is seeking whom?

# 20. Two AM

*"...a new kind of loneliness..."*

*Bumblebees (Voyage) by ABBA*

is a lonely hour.
Half is asleep.
Half is not awake.
Only the darkness plays
with the darkness as its prey.
Two AM
is a lonely hour.
Only the dark
holds the memories
of the bees and tigers gone.
Only the dark
holds the impressions
of sense and sensibility too.
Two AM
is a lonely hour.
To know that all you know
is dying slowly away.
To know that only you will ever know
that you were you.
Two AM
is a lonely hour.

## 21. The Dead Poet

Do my words
make your soul sing?
Do my thoughts
echo in your mind
long after they ring?

Are my words
like the gentle moon?
Do they tide your heart
with emotions that ebb and flow
and make you swoon?

No? Asked the lonesome Poet.
The world turned languidly.
Does it matter that words
are strung in gold or ink?
--was the quiet apathy.

"Well then, my life is useless."
the obscure Poet said.
"My words be corpses
feeding in a lonely grave.
I may as well be dead."

# 22. Remember Me

You remembered me even
when you forgot yourself
in the throes of youth and silly bravado.
When love was a music of drums
and time was inconsequential.
Life's burdens were a background hum.
And death always at someone else's doorstep.
Romance was holding hands,
and giggles and silly murmurings
under giant faraway stars that shone only for us.
Each day, I asked, "Did you forget my love?"
"Of course not," she said.

Did you remember me then
when you forgot yourself
caring for our children and paying bills?
When love was a music of flutes
and time a ticking clock.
As the hum got louder
and death passed close.
Holding hands only to pretend
during our daily fights

and petty arguments,
bitter breakups and sweet makeups.
Each day, I asked, “Do you remember, my love?”
“Of course, I do,” she said.

Remember me
when you forget yourself.
When love becomes life
and time a tedious thing.
Death’s sweet breath is upon us.
In the debris of time,
memory lay as rubble.
Torn fragments,
some missing a start, some an end.
Some the reason why
and gradually the who.
Holding hands through pain and comfort.
Each day, I ask, “Do you remember, my love?”
“Remember what?” she said.

# 23. The Song of a Cat – A Fragment

Dear Cat, sit by me.
For this moment, leave all be.
My little one, just you and me.

The world shall speed on
in a morbid feeding frenzy.
We'll gaze up at the blue
with not a thing to do.

The man in the corner finds
a million ways to make a million more.
Our little twine binds
our happiness to make us soar.

The man in the corner builds
great walls, hard and comfortless.
A box to leap in and out
is all we want as our bless.

The man in the corner thinks
nature is in his lab to test.
Our eye is on the mind and so we sit.
Nature is in us and we in it.

The man in the corner amends
rules and regulations to bend.
O little Cat, we stand on our stone,
the leaves and wet mud make it our happy throne.

O little one, little Cat
bounce and leap and tumble
O little Cat, dear Cat
asleep at last with a soft rumble.

# 24. The Artic Storm

He shielded his eyes against the snow.
There was no horizon.
Earth and sky had folded.
The sun had deserted the land.
Siku, he called.
She whined in reply.
Her warm nose in his icy hand.
The key is to stay slant and low,
bend but don't yield,
he told his dog wisely.
This is how one stays warm.
This is how one weathers a storm.

# 25. A Calendar of Incense

The King said:

Hear the kneeducts roar!
with smelly crossmack of lies
prickly crabs of sixbunnies
empowered with thunderous sunrise
and a gaggle of right-wing dunnies
incumbency flies gumbly
'tis the juby whitewash
and foss the grey melons
kittled with red radosh
giant and fosty megallans.
Throw the allies and the fiscs!
Poke diggly gettlesticks
besides the podly proprium
louder than the other moontics
motter the pandemonium.
Hear the kneeducts roar!
The King doth swell and soar!

The People said:

Oh, hear the wise King speak!
Our wise ruler!
Bow to him and wish him well!
Give him taxes! Give him levies!
Oh, hear our King speak!
Our wise benefactor!
We bow to him! We wish him well!
Mark our calendar of incense!
Pay him our dues!
Pay him our respect!
We, the people, have the common sense!

## 26. Meesa

Time is an old old man.
They called him Meesa
for his big flamboyant moustache.
I called him nosey,
because I always saw him peering,
poking around,
looking for something he could eat.
For Meesa had an appetite.
And what an appetite it was!
He would devour
just about anything,
a bird or two,
a tree or a snail,
or even just an old shoe.

Every day he would come a-calling
for his daily tidbits.
And I would hunt high and low,
in and out for a little treat.
An old book or a table
that he would wolf down like meat.
A blackened dish on the stove

or a mouldy curtain.
A useless memory
or an uncertain feeling.
He wasn't very particular
what he would consume
so long as he was fed
satisfactorily.
And Meesa would leave only to be back
on the morrow.

Little by little he ate.
Coming back for more and more.
Soon I was running out of things
that would keep his hunger at bay.
He fed on my teeth.
He did not spare
my eyes or a nail
or even my straggly hair.
My blood dwindled away.
My muscles shrunk to threads.
He snacked on my memories
till I had to write down my name.
And life became a gentle balance
of dignity and shame.

He suckled on my hope
and gobbled up all my courage.
My mind was a gaping hole
until there was naught to feed him
                                        but for my empty soul.

# 27. A Land Without a Home

One day, the little boy looked up from his toy horse.

He looked at his house. He looked at the sky.

He looked at the trees and simply could not fathom the what, how or why.

He looked at his mama, with his sister on her hip, toiling at the stove.

"O mama, what is this world?" he said. "Tell me where it be."

His busy mama replied, "It's house and work and money, my love."

The boy paused at the world and looked but did not see.

He stepped out into the garden and walked the path, hesitantly.

In the corner of the lane stood a majestic mango tree.

Old and gnarly, heavy with leaves and fruits, with a shade cool and dim.

"O tree, what is this world?" he said. "Tell me where it be."

"A breeze without a wind, my boy." The leaves whispered softly back at him.

On the boy went till he saw a cow that stood and stood and stood in a field.

She swished her tail and chewed her grass and swished her tail and chewed her grass.

"O cow, what is this world?" he said. "Tell me where it be."

"Patience without waiting, O little one." Slowly and gently, said she.

He walked on and on and on till it got too hot and sat down tiredly.

He looked at the sun and the sun at him and thought he could ask again.

"O sun, what is this world?" he said. "Tell me where it be."

"Time without a sunrise." Said the sun as he shone down at him, brilliantly.

He turned off the road and headed into the trees; tall, straight and bent.

Perhaps the answer be ahead in the forest so he said to himself and so on he went.

He walked on and on until there stood an anthill.

"O ant, O ant, what is this world?" he said. "Tell me where it be."

"Strength without power." Without a pause they chanted in unison.

He sat on a log, dangling his feet in a stream, and rolling his question.

A bee buzzed by his ear and heard him softly mention.

"O bee," he said. "What is this world? Tell me where it be."

"Fragrance without a flower." Hummed the bee.

"There's nothing more than that for me."

He scratched his nose and was about to leave.

When he saw monkey swinging up and down in a tree.

"O monkey," He called. "What is this world? Tell me where it be."

"Joy without laughter, of course." Monkey twittered happily.

The boy skipped along on and on till the edge of the land.

He stood and looked at the sea that swished and swashed at his feet.

"O sea, what is this world?" He shouted out. "Tell me where it be."

"Action without activity," said the sea, splashing him thoroughly.

The little boy turned his path and walked on and on till the twilight peeped into the sky.

He gazed up as the moon sailed up and the clouds scurried by.

"O moon, what is this world?" he asked. "Tell me where it be."

"Rest without sleep, my boy." Said the moon dreamily.

The little boy didn't stop till the mountains rose up quietly.

The mountain swirled its mists, bent low and rumbled softly.

"O boy, what is this world? Tell me what you see."

The boy paused and smiled and paused and smiled and looked up at the mountain.

"A land without a home, of course. A land without a home. This is the place for me."

# 28. The Shadow That Was Him

And in the light, he saw a shadow.
It had started softly at his brow.
Until it spread one day and took his shape
and followed him everywhere in his wake.

Sometimes it silently flapped and waved.
Sometimes it mischievously mimicked and aped.
Sometimes it tagged along behind
and at times he followed it blind.

Sometimes it grew long and stretched out.
Sometimes it was just a tiny spout.
He could not outrun or hide.
It simply would never leave his side.

Bright lights only made it lurk.
And the day came when light made him shirk.
And thus, it hovered around him
till the only way out was to give in.

And so, the darkness slowly grew around
as it swallowed and engulfed without a sound.
And took him for its own, down to the last limb.
Till naught was left but the shadow that was him.

# 29. Hope's a Bitch

"Is she now?" he said.
"Dream your dream.
Hope your tomorrow.
They are yours to take."
He smiled and said.

"No"
I said.
"Hope's a bitch."
Wishes, dreams and future lies
are flimsy dust in sunny rays.
And there I stood
firm and still.

Yet she wriggled
and niggled her way
and in a dark corner,
an unwanted hope arose.
A tiny spark that grew
bright as day.
For what is life
without a hope.

But what is hope
that never blossoms,
never sees fruit.
But in the darkness
laughs you silly.
You hear it chuckle.
You hear it sneer.
*She's just sensitive.*
*A silly little dear.*
And then it is smashed
one fine day
and gone away.
But then the shreds…
are only you.
Hope is whole.
And on its merry way
to ensnare another
and make its prey.

O why did I
dream my dream?
O why did I
hope my tomorrow?
"No"

I said.
Hope’s a bitch.
“Not again.”
I said.
And there I stood
firm and still
hopeless and damned
vacant and still.

# 30. The Wall

Sitting
    staring
        at the walls.
Blinking
    darkening
        inner walls.
Colours
    races
        building walls.
Borders
    countries
        dividing walls.
Killings
    violence
        closing walls.
Loving
    weddings
        making walls.
Dying
    losing
        breaking walls.

# 31. There is a Poem Stuck in Me

There is a poem stuck in me.
It's niggling and wriggling just below the surface.
I feel it there, does it feel me?
There is a poem stuck in me.
Is it about a little boy, a mountain, or a sad winter's day?
Is it an old memory that I need to say?
It's welling up inside of me, it struggles to get out.
It's leaping and kicking all my organs about.
There is a poem stuck in me.
My hair tumbles up and my eyes bubble around.
Little bits of rhymes burp out, the words spilling to the ground.
It jiggles and tinkles in my ear, a strand of music bursts from my tongue.
A fragment here, a bit of verse there, or an ode that is sung.
It shudders and twitches and trembles and jerks.
Little demons emerge from the darkness where it lurks.
It giggles and chortles and snorts and sniggers.
Anything as far out as in, it uses as triggers.
Will it take days or hours or minutes to still?
And to write it on paper, with pen or quill.

There is a poem written by me.
At last, innocent and true, on the paper, it lay.
All quiet and peaceful like a sigh after a squall.
I thought I had had something to say.
But lo! It was not me at all.
T'was the poem that had had a field day.

# 32. The Jasmine Tea

**Jassi**

ah ah Ah AH!
With a gasp and a sigh,
they lay side by side.
Who knew that it could be
so satisfying to live a lie?
Jassi moaned contentedly,
and snuggled closer to the bed.
She knew she had to get up.
There never was enough time.
There never was anything said.
As he stirred, she understood
and got to her slender white feet,
moving languidly to the
kitchen to make some tea.
Payment for the afternoon treat.
She boiled the milk and water.
A splendid and fragrant brew.
A special tea of dark leaves
infused with the scent of white jasmine,
one to melt away the blue.

He sipped his tea slowly
and watched the other
as she straightened her clothes,
her hair, and all the things
that made her a wife and a mother.
His dark presence melted away.
But a voice in her head
told her he would be back.
He longed for her, it said,
not just for her bed.
Jassi hummed as she
went through her chores.
Cooking and cleaning,
stacking up the toys,
and washing all the underclothes.
Soon her children would be
back from their school
and soon her dull husband.
The evening would drag interminably
between tantrums and a bumbling old fool.

**A New Life**

She hadn't known him
when she had first arrived
at the monstrous steel plant
with her husband
as a newly-wed bride.
It had all seemed exciting,
the huge buildings,
all the noise and smells,
from enormous machinery
and really high ceilings.
She hadn't known him
when she had first met
the other wives in the colony
who were kindly at first
and didn't see her as a threat.
They showed her around.
Everywhere they could go.
Around the steel plant.
Around the quarters,
the markets and the bangle store.
And then her life got busy.

One child and yet another.
Getting to know her husband,
keeping up with her in-laws,
and getting to know herself as a mother.
The more she got to know
the more she saw
that the steel walls
were closing in around her
as wife, mother and daughter-in-law.
Her sole reprieve at first
were the other wives in the colony
who called out to her,
Jassi, sweet Jassi,
come and have some tea.
They never forgot her
wherever they went.
In the markets
or with each other
all the time that was spent.

**A New Threat**

Soon she was to see
that the other wives
were much more than
just housework
and intimate family ties.
One afternoon when she visited
her friend in the colony.
To her surprise, she
was engrossed in making
a strange man some tea.
They looked at each other
while they were waiting
for her friend to pour
the thick hot brew
with something new stirring.
She forgot all about it
till the time her in-laws
left for a wedding.
And one hot afternoon,
he began his visits.
She looked out of the window.
The sun blazed down.
Everyone was indoors

or working at the steel plant.
Not a soul was around.
Her husband would be busy
chatting his time away
in the great big godown.
This was the time when
her lover would make his way.
Now the voice in her head
hummed happily.
There was something to look forward to.
For every quiet afternoon
she waited for him excitedly.
She knew he had stopped
visiting the other silly wives.
In that remote quarters
that made up their home
and their solitary lives.

**A New Voice**

Then another voice in her head
stirred in its beginnings.
What would happen
when her cranky old in-laws
returned to those cramped livings?
Would he then stop
visiting her every day?
Would he then return
to all those silly wives?
And she would not have a say.
As the day neared
when her in-laws
were to return,
the voice in her head
grew louder for its cause.
She got more and more listless,
and even the silly wives,
who never thought
beyond housework
and intimate family ties,
began to notice
that Jassi, sweet Jassi,
seemed quite not herself.

In vain did they call,
Jassi, come have some tea.
Come to the markets.
Come to the bangle store.
But Jassi, sweet Jassi,
shook her soft head
and did not listen anymore.
And the silly wives laughed.
How long will she have him.
He will be back with us,
before the tea brews.
It's just a silly whim.

**A New Tea**

As the day neared
when her in-laws were to return.
She could see he knew.
She could see him eager.
The rise of a new yearn.
And, she, back to the
the daily grind of chores
with her children and husband
And her mother-in-law's
many aches and sores.

And so on his last visit,
he came in the same.
No remorse, no regret.
Just another cup of tea.
Just another afternoon game.
ah ah Ah AH!
With a gasp and a sigh,
they lay side by side.
Who knew that it could be
so satisfying to live a lie?
She boiled the milk and water
and took her time with the tea.
A special one with dark leaves
that drain the scent of white jasmine,
one to set them both free.
This time she sat down
with him for the tea.
He looked surprised at first
to see two cups instead
of just the one for a fee.

He took the cup from her
and watched her slipping girlhood.
He began to drink the hot tea
that seemed extra special but
too late, he saw her smile and understood.
Before he could finish
the thought in his head,
his cup slipped to the floor.
With a gasp and a sigh,
he dropped dead.

# 33. Voyage

Little traveller, how goes your voyage?
Be it like a ship?
Setting off in cheer and drink,
riding fury of storms
and desperate mannings,
losing a crew here and there,
arriving at some unknown port,
beaten and bruised
or stabbed with a hole and sunken down deep.

Little traveller, how goes your voyage?
Be it like snow?
From a cold and ashen sky
soft soft and noiseless
gliding gliding and floating
never on its own steam
blown hither and thither
up again at times
and resting down finally
merging and lost to eternity.

Little traveller, how goes your voyage?
Be it like rain?

Bursting from a storm
with light and loud thunder
lashing and surging
rushing to its end
splattering to the ground.

Little traveller, how goes your voyage?
Be it like the tide?
Rushing up from the sea
with a great deal of urgency
rising up like a bird
pretending to be away
with a splash and show
and then dragging back uselessly.

# 34. Would You Know Time?

Would you know time?
If it weren't for your clock.
Would you know time?
If it weren't for the sun.
Would you know time?
If it weren't for the tiding seas.
Or the buds that bloom.
Clouds that breeze.
Or nature's wintery gloom.
Would you know time?
If it weren't for your aging face.
And the slowly withering body,
creeping, begging its way to grace.

# 35. Sands on a Beach

*I'm Nobody! Who are you? (260)*

*Emily Dickinson - 1830-1886*

He stood, lonely and quiet,
amidst the sunny fun and frolic.
Looking out at the sea
with blank vacant frog eyes,
a lifeguard, alert and vigil.

Day after day he stood
quiet and still.
Looking out at the sea
a lifeguard, alert and vigil.

He knew every grain of sand
on that undulating beach.
Sifting and shifting
beneath all the happy feet.
With each incessant wave
that arose, the sands
were pushed ashore
or dragged to the depths,
bogged down by currents,

thrust to new lands and old,
there and back again,
over and over again.

Pointlessly in the flow.
Each grain thinking it was only one.
Each thinking it has a plan, a goal.
Sifting and shifting
surging and receding
to new lands and old
there and back again
over and over again.

He stood, lonely and quiet
looking out at the sea
at the arms that flayed
between the waves
and disappeared as people cried.
Shouting and pointing
and rushing up to him.
"No matter," he said.
"One is alive and one is dead
there and back again
over and over again."

He stood, lonely and quiet
amidst the panic and despair
looking out at the sea
with blank vacant frog eyes,
a lifeguard, alert and vigil.

# 36. "Take Me!"

I cried out.
"Take me, Sir!"
He looked at me dolefully.
And what he saw
I could also see.
An old old lady.
Grey grizzled hair.
Mottled hands.
A body beyond care.
And in a goddamned hurry.

And so he turned away
leaving me to do my time
to shed my soul's cover
before he came back for mine.

# 37. The Gravedigger

"Dig dig dig,"
said the gravedigger.
"I have many more to go.
Corpses lining up.
Bodies for a great big show.
Dig dig dig,"
said the gravedigger.
"Mustn't stop a minute.
There's too a-many now.
Till all are holed up in it.
The skies are grey.
And the light turning dark.
There's another motley array.
Here's another that's quite stark.
And lo! here's one that thinks it's fun.
He's played merry with a getaway gun.
Dig dig dig,"
said the gravedigger.
"The soil is hard and cold.
She's long waited and watched
as the greedy got bold.

And so her army has torched
the blights with diseases and quakes
till each last one of them shakes."
"What about me?
Feed feed feed,"
said the feeder.
"The earth's so hungry today.
She's had her fill.
And yet she wants her bouquet.
She out for a deadly kill."

## 38. Dare to Dream

I dared to dream
one day
the earth would reclaim
all its own.
For what did we offer but
killings, killings and more killings.
Eating, eating and more eating.
Only to starve all else.
Crowding up remote mountains,
leaving foul carcasses,
mixing excretions,
slimy oils and toxic plastics.
All for money,
all for greed.
Did the earth ever ask for money?
Did the deer graze for a fee?
Did the April showers charge for drops?
I dared to dream
one day
the earth would reclaim
all its own.

And so, one day, it did,
silently and without contempt,
all that she gave for free.
I dared to dream
one day
that I could claim
this change.
And in the dark,
a voice laughed softly.
Did you dare to dream
that this was you?
The earth is just
another ball in space
another toy in space
one of so many.
Your dream is mine.
And so are you.
I dreamed your dream.
I am you.

# 39. Waterfalls

In faraway Japan,
one day,
I stood at the bottom,
of a mighty waterfall,
watching it cascading,
thundering and plunging,
splashing all the way down.
Oh, it looked so very busy
like it meant a purpose.
But would it not all
just go down to the sea
to rise up again
in faint phantom clouds
only to be back as rain
and join the mighty waterfall
thundering and plunging,
splashing all the way down,
some day
in faraway Japan.

# 40. The Vodka Song

One little vodka, what can it do?
What can it do?
One little vodka, I think I'll have two.
I think I'll have two.

Two little vodka, can you still see ?
Can you still see?
Two little vodka, let us have three.
Let us have three.

Three little vodka, need one to go.
Need one to go.
Three little vodka, round it up to four.
Round it up to four.

Four little vodka, here comes the high.
Here comes the high.
Four little vodka, let's give it up at five.
Give it up at five.

Five little vodka, just a few more licks.
Just a few more licks.
Five little vodka, it's a merry six.
It's a merry six.

Six little vodka, all aboard for heaven.
All aboard for heaven.
Six little vodka, chalk it up to seven.
Chalk it up to seven.

Seven little vodka, everyone's my mate.
Everyone's my mate.
Seven little vodka, bottoms up to eight.
Bottoms up to eight.

Eight little vodka, this will do just fine.
This will do just fine.
Eight little vodka, let us stop at nine.
Let us stop at nine.

Nine little vodka, feeling very zen.
Feeling very zen.
Nine little vodka, I think I had ten.
I think I had ten.

# About the Author

Vandana has had a long career writing and editing technical documentation for several multi-national companies. In recent years, she turned to teaching English and reading. She writes poems and articles in her leisure time, which she inflicts without mercy on her family and friends. Her one regret is that in most of her stories and poems someone ends up dead.

Vandana lives in Bangalore with cats and a garden.

www.ingramcontent.com/pod-product-compliance
Lightning Source LLC
Chambersburg PA
CBHW020020260726
48782CB00024B/165

*9798892772327*